Order this book online at www.trafford.com
or email orders@trafford.com

Most Trafford titles are also available at major online book retailers.

Printed in Victoria, BC, Canada.

ISBN: 978-1-4269-1945-9 (sc)
ISBN: 978-1-4269-1946-6 (hc)

Library of Congress Control Number: 2009913208

*Our mission is to efficiently provide the world's finest, most comprehensive book publishing
service, enabling every author to experience success. To find out how to publish your book, your
way, and have it available worldwide, visit us online at www.trafford.com*

Trafford rev. 1/06/10

 www.trafford.com

North America & international
toll-free: 1 888 232 4444 (USA & Canada)
phone: 250 383 6864 ♦ fax: 812 355 4082

TO MY ENTIRE LOVING FAMILY
AND ALL MY FRIENDS
DONNA LEE (ROBERT) GREGG

Contents

Biographical Information

I always liked to put my thoughts on paper in rhymes
All of the thoughts I had hidden in the back of my mind
I like to write easy to understand poems with no punctuation
If one of my poems helps someone through a bad situation
Or makes someone smile from reading one of my poems
Or helps one person make a good choice because of a poem
I enjoy writing true short story poems of family and friends
I also love making up my own pretend poems with happy ends
I wrote a book named The Angels Who saved the alphabet
I hope will make it more fun for children to learn the alphabet
I am hoping it will be published sometime early in 2010
Perhaps one of you reading this book will buy one of them

My Miracle from heaven was one of my best poems
Lilly is my great grandchild and one of my favorite poems
You see I am 75 years old and for a time I almost died
In the hospital they over medicated me so I almost died
I thank God for my heart doctor he found the problem
I have no doubt that I am alive just because of him
Lilly had not been born yet when I wrote this for her
I will write many more now that she is here just for her
Now you understand that thanking God is a must for her

A Slice of Heaven

A slice of heaven is to hear a new born cry
It is like the loving look in mothers eyes
A slice of heaven is to make children happy
Let them know your love whatever happens
A slice of heaven is to never strike in anger
And to always try to keep them from danger
All of their laughter will be thanks to you
For all of the things for them you will do
A slice of heaven is to sing them lullabies
And wishing they never had to say bye-bye
Put all these slices of heaven together
And you will soon have their love forever
All the slices came from Angel Food Cakes
That all the children came together to bake
Angels came down to give them the ingredients
God gave us the chances to be the recipients
The more slices of heaven we earn in life
The more God will help us go toward the light

A Gift for My Heart

A gift for my heart will not cost money
It will not have to be coated in honey
You do not have to shop at any place
And it will not take up needed space
Do not worry about it if it will not fit me
Do not wrap with bows for me to see
A gift for my heart is really easy to give
My family helps my heart want to live
A gift for my heart is also easy to find
A gift of giving respect and being kind
Of warm hugs and sweet loving smiles
For these I would walk for many miles
The best gift for my heart is my family
Everyone should have a loving family

Thank you God for mine

If Clouds Had Cell Phones

I think I really should be cleaning up the kitchen
But something else came alone and caught my attention
I looked out the window and found the sun had disappeared
I knew that meant we had some storms about to appear
Everyone knows how much I love to watch the clouds
To me it is like each one of them is so strong and proud
And they have a very great story to tell all of their own
It could be great if they had a way for them to have cell phones
To tell their story before the storm blows them far from home
Or finds themselves separated from the others and all alone

Home in the Clouds

If only I could fly high like a dove
And reach those fluffy clouds up above
I would land on one and take my time
To stake out a claim and make it mine
After I build my house I would eagerly
Share my home and cloud with Eagles
Of course I would always be on vacation
And my cloud would always be in motion
As wonderful as it is to have such dreams
I know it would not be peaches and cream
A tornado could come along and wipe me out
It would throw my home and cloud all about
So maybe I will build my home here on earth
Because this is where my Mother gave me birth
I really believe God will help keep me safe
As long as I can truly keep up the faith
I will go on trusting my God with my life
Until I am called upon to go to the light

A Big White Cloud

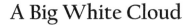

Out the window I watched a big white cloud
I wanted so badly to scream right out loud
Please do not just pass over this little town
Please stay here so we can hang around
There are many things I would like to say
And I am sure it will take more than a day
To tell you about all of the things in my life
That has happened since I became a wife
The best is I had two wonderful children
They gave me four wonderful grandchildren
Maybe I had better wait for another day
To tell you all of the things I wanted to say
You had better hurry to your destination
Because according to my very good estimation
There is a very ugly big dark and angry storm
And it looks like it is feeling very full of scorn
It looks like it would love to blow you away
So I will save my story to tell you another day

Clouds

Anyone who knows me knows I love the clouds
Sometimes I can look up in the sky and be proud
To be an American who is lucky enough to live
In a country that knows how to not take but to give
If any other Country suffers from a natural disaster
We are one of the first to arrive on the scene after
We will always try to help wherever it is needed
And we will all try to help until we have succeeded
Next time you are out side looking up at the clouds
Please make sure you take the time to be very proud

Rainbows

There are many stories and myths about Rainbows
The facts that there are pretty colors all in a row
And some say there is a pot of Gold at the very end
But most people do not know there are really no ends
A Rainbow is really an endless very perfect circle
Another one of Gods many very lovely Miracles
Do you think that funny little Men could be so bold
As to cut a Rainbow in half to have a place for Gold
Who cares how as long as they are able to find a way
For us to keep looking for a Pot of Gold every day

The reason I wrote Smooth out the Wrinkles
I have met many people whose life is like Wrinkles
They do not seem to know how to smooth them out
I know I have been there and I know what it's about
It took all my strength to get back my get up and scat
My get up and scat helped me to smooth out my life
And my Faith in God and family made me love my life

Smooth Out the Wrinkles

If you ever wished you had never been born
Because your life seems all wrinkled and torn
Smooth out the wrinkles with a kind warm heart
A kind warm heart can mend all of the torn parts
If family and friends help you back on your feet
You will be very lucky and will not except defeat
Even if you do not have the best of good health
With loving family and friends you have wealth
If you are lucky enough to have some children
And even luckier like me and have grandchildren
Then your life is already much richer than some
And your chance of being alone is little to none
So if you ever do wish you had never been born
Know this is a better world because you were born

I wrote Unconditional Love because I have so much of it
Sometimes people take advantage of it to test me on it
Thank God I still have all that love so I passed the test
But there are so many people who cannot pass the test
That can make a family soon to fall apart at the seams
If you take advantage of love remember what it may mean
Then you may find that some of your family may be mean

Unconditional Love

Unconditional love from someone should be appreciated
Never take it for granted for fear it may get depreciated
Because someone loves you know matter what you do
Do not think you can do really bad things and get love to
Unconditional love can go conditional if you are too bad
There may be limits if you go too far and that would be sad
Sad because unconditional love comes so seldom in life
So earn that love and make your life shine with sunlight
Then you will make unconditional love last for a lifetime
 If you want to have unconditional love keep this in mind

I Do Not Have a Clue

I do not have a clue why some days
I can do what I want in so many ways
And then some days seem to fall apart
As soon as I try to get a really good start
I know there must be a really good reason
But for me it seems like the four seasons
The winter never knows when to stop
Spring is waiting to send up new crops
Summer is hoping to drive spring away
Fall never wants summer to be able to stay
It is always trying to keep winter away
If Mother Nature does not have a clue
Why should I think that I could have a clue

I wrote Hate can Destroy You for one reason only
Hate can destroy you and you wind up being lonely
It is my hope that people who hates learns to forgive
Not to forgive makes a heart cold and is no way to live
I hope your heart can lose the hate and learn to forgive

Hate Can Destroy You

Hate can and will destroy most of your body and brain
It can come undetected to some people like a big rain
To much of it will cause huge damaging flash flooding
Hate can cause beautiful gardens to stop their budding
It can also be the cause of a lot of relationships failing
Hate should be picked up and thrown over the railing
Then when it crashes and it breaks into pieces galore
You could look up and see the opening of many doors
There are so many ways to get rid of hate what can I say
I will cut this poem short and tell you more another day

I wrote stories about Fun Stories as a Child because
I had a happy childhood but there were a few pauses
My sister was three and a half years older than myself
Growing up she was always playing with someone else
But then when we grew up we became very very close
We married great guys and had great kids for us both
My brother made up for me not seeing a lot of my sister
He had so much fun playing many tricks on his baby sister

Fun Stories as a Child

When we were young my Brother was caught smoking
And of course that was against the rules for us to smoke
So my Father decided to teach him a really good lesson
He sat him down made him light a big cigar and said Son
You will get so sick you may not ever smoke another one
Little did he know the plan was going to backfire on Dad
Because what cigar smoke did to my Dad was really sad
He was very sick for at least three days then he was mad
Because smoke did not bother my Brother like it did Dad

Fun Stories as a Child #2

There was a Rooster that made a fun story for me
When I went to the farm there was a Rooster after me
That always came after me when I went out to play
It seemed to always know when I went too far away
To get back to the house before the Rooster got to me
Then I would scream for help and out came my Granny
She ran off the Rooster and said it would soon be stew
And sure enough the very next day we had chicken stew

Fun Stories as a Child #3

This is a fun story of my two children as children
Their father worked nights so I put them to bed when
They were not sleepy so they would watch the door
So when I went to the kitchen to do the dishes and more
They sneaked into the living room to play a trick on me
We laughed so hard when my chair pillow was nowhere to see
We laughed harder the next night when my chair was missing
From then on we laughed just talking about chairs I missed

Fun Stories as a Child #4

When I was old enough to fix my own butter and bread
When Mom wanted to fix it I said no I wanted too instead
I started fixing my own peanut butter and jelly sandwich
Then I fixed my own open faced peanut butter sandwiches
They were beautiful when I put my artistic ability to them
There was not a spot without peanut butter and jelly on them
Dad would say look at that and steel it when I looked away
I looked back and Dad had a big bite out of my bread that day
He started a habit that lasted the rest of his life what can I say

Fun Stories as a Child #5

My whole family used to tease me about potatoes
They said when I was very young I called them tatoes
If we went to dinner I did not want pepper on my tatoes
I got older and they had baked potatoes on the dinner table
It took me a long time to peel and mash them just right
I had to have butter all over them so they were so nice
Then all of a sudden the whole family was very quiet
I looked and they were looking at my plate with delight
From then on family dinners had a minute of silence so
No one would miss me fixing my potatoes up just so

A Good Day

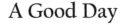

I think I will put a smile on my face
I think it will be one of those days
If I make sure I am really very nice
Do all of my chores and do them right
Mom will be so very very proud of me
Dad will hug and bounce me on his knee
We will go out to get my favorite Pizza
They said I could invite my friend Lisa
When we get home we eat ice cream
When I go to bed they say sweet dreams
A kiss and a hug and a sweet good night
Such a good day I am so glad I did right

Nap Time is something all Moms Know about
When nap time comes most moms come out
They know if they do not get their work done
The kids wake up and the work never gets done
I am sure all moms on the planet knows nap time
They look forward to having a little down time
You need to forget bringing out mops and brooms
The kitchen and dishes and all of the other rooms
So take a deep breath and get back to the nap room

Nap Time

I think its time for you to take a nap
I see two very sleepy eyes under that cap
While you sleep I will be quiet as a mouse
As I go about my chores and clean the house
When I finish cleaning I will wash clothes
Then I will water the lawn with the hose
After I water the lawn I will bake a cake
After I bake a cake some icing I will make
Then I will fix for your dinner a pot roast
I will fix the potatoes you love the most
Goodness just talking about what I will do
Made me so tired I decided to nap with you

Did you ever wonder was another fun poem
I did wonder why grownups wrote poems
About Humpty Dumpty having a great fall
Because grownups let him fall off the wall
They probably made Pinnochios nose grow
They made him out of wood so his nose grows
It was fun and so was the cradle on that limb
I would never put a baby in a cradle on a limb
I wanted to fly around in Santas slay with him

Did You Ever Wonder

As a child I wondered how Santa could fly
And why Pinnochios nose grows when he lies
Why Humpty Dumpty would want to set on a wall
When he knew he might have a really great fall
Why would anyone put a cradle in the tree top
And let the wind come and make the cradle rock
They know what will happen if that limb breaks
Why in the world put a Baby there for heaven sakes
Sometimes I did not see how grown ups think
Because to let that Baby fall really does stink
Did you ever wonder about some of these things

Spread Honey

If people only knew how easy it would be
To spread honey around just like honey bees
The world would be a sweeter place to live
Then maybe children could learn how to give
Instead of always fighting with their siblings
They learn how to share some of their things
They learn more about how to love not hate
If everyone felt the same it would be great
It matters not what color your skin may be
What really matters are if you are able to see
That the world would be a wonderful place
If we can love and look each other in the face
We can teach our children how to have faith
And live their life like there is no time to waste
With God in their heart how easy it would be
To spread honey around just like a honey bee

Children Laughing and Smiling

When you see and hear your children laughing and smiling
It makes you want to forever keep all of them from crying
When the day is over and you finally get them all to eat
That is when the fun starts in trying to get them in their seat
Every thing is fine as long as the meat gravy and potatoes
Comes without peas and carrots or spinach and tomatoes
So you say eat your vegetables or go without your dessert
They eat their vegetables because not to get dessert would hurt
Then they fight over which one has to wash or dry dishes
I walk out of the kitchen hoping if they toss them no one misses
When they are done the oldest ones do homework for school
The younger ones are tearing up a toy so they want a tool
I am pulling my hair out hoping the time will soon be bedtime
Then I will have made it the whole day without losing my mind
When I finally get all of them out of the tub from taking a bath
And the older ones are settled in and the youngest is on my lap
She is waiting to see if you will read her a story or sing her a song
And I am so tired I hope that she gets really sleepy before long
After they are all asleep I tuck them in and kiss them all goodnight
I leave their rooms and close the doors and hope they sleep tight
I miss all of their voices so much I cannot wait for the next day
So I can live everything that happened today in the very same way

People Who Act Like Fools I wrote just for fun
All young people love to act like fools just for fun
They have so much fun playing the part of the fool
It makes me want to play with them being a fool
Even if I am 75 years old I never get to old for fun
When you get my age you get to have a lot more fun
If you want to get my age and still love to have fun
You have earned the right to be a fool so go for fun

People Who Act Like Fools

Most people who act like they are real fools
Are people who love to have fun not be a real fool
Real fools are the people who call everyone else fools
Little do they know that all the people they call a fool
Knows they are really the fools for calling them fools
Now that I have everyone confused about who is a fool
I admit I love to have fun so if that makes me a fool
Then I love being a fool how about you are you a fool

I wrote Do Not Cheat or Lie because so many do
I have lived a long life and watched so many who do
I hate what it does to all the children that it hurts
They really are teaching their children to do it first
The children wind up thinking this is normal behavior
Maybe they were taught this is all normal behavior
I do hope they will fall in love and not cheat or lie
Then they will teach their children to not cheat or lie

Do Not Cheat Or Lie

I think when married people cheat and lie
A part of their ability to really Love dies
They are teaching their children a way to live
It will make it impossible for them to give
The children will learn how to lie and cheat
In a fair game they cannot stand to get beat
They do not understand to cheat is wrong
Their friends will not be friends for long
When they find true Love it may be too late
To do right by their Love and be a good mate
I wish the parents would learn how to play fair
Then the children will know they really do care
They could teach them how to live a good life
Then for the right to live free they will fight

When I Feel Down

To My Husband

When I feel very unloved and very sad
And someone hurts me and makes me mad
I sometimes wish I had made better choices
Then I close my eyes and realize I hear voices
The voices are coming from my two children
And they are talking to my four grandchildren
That is a sound that came from Heaven above
It was a sound born from two people in love
So really my family is among the very best
And my husband and I are really very blessed

My Dear Mother

To My Dear Mother

She was a very shy and very lovely little lady
She made sure she always took care of her babies
While we were growing up she was always there
She worked hard to be sure the table was not bare
Even though she had to work away from home
She tried so hard to make sure we were not alone
There was only one of her but three of us children
Needless to say it is hard trying to be a Mother Hen
When your chicks are running all around the place
I am surprised she could keep a smile on her face
There is not enough room in this Poem for me to say
Things about my Mom that would take more than a day
Matter of fact I am not sure I could get it in one book
Because she could tell a story with just one little look

My Two Best Friends

Abby and Joan just happens to be their names
I want them both to know I love them the same
We met when we all began working together
As the years went by our friendship got better
Every once in a while all three of us got mad
But most of the time we were able to stay glad
Most of the time we enjoyed working together
The times we were able to all go out was better
Were all retired now and busy with our families
I am glad I have more time with all my family
But I do really miss not seeing Joan and Abby
To see them more often would make me happy
Until that happens God be with Joan and Abby

Love You Both

Night Sky

There is nothing more beautiful than the night sky
Sometime it is enough to make you wonder why
You look up in the sky and watch all of the stars
And wonder how far it might be from here to Mars
Who really cares just how far it is from here too there
Except astronauts who want to go to Mars really care
If I was a young astronaut I would want to go to Mars
Be up in space with them flying all around in the stars
I always wished I had been born one hundred years later
I would be born in the space age that would be greater

I think the Giant was the hardest poem I have ever wrote
I was in the kitchen when all that horrible news broke
I ran to the TV and watched horrified at the smoking Tower
I was also watching as the second plane struck the Tower
When I realized how many people were dying I just lost it
I would watch TV and cry then watch and pray about it
Later I wrote the Giant and did not stop until I finished it

The Giant

A great brave and protective Giant awoke with an angry cry
On the day they bombed Pearl Harbor and so many of us died
The Giant knew all he had to do was to gather all his men
And he only had to ask his great nation to back him too win
His great nation the United States of America came together
So now we know when united we stand we will survive forever
Now on September 11 2001 terrorist invaded our shores
They killed thousands of us and hurt us right down to the core
Now the Giant we call the United States of America is ready
The Giant is ready willing and able to help the people stand steady
What the terrorist does not understand our flag flies high
Our faith in God keeps us strong even if some of us have to die
We will not give up our freedom and the love of our nation
Our Military has gathered in force to stand at their station
You terrorist cannot hide forever and we will take you out
God Bless America Land That We Love that is what we are about

So Many Things to Say

There are so many things I have wanted to say
To say them all would take more than a day
On September 11 2001 evil came to our shores
We did not have time to close all our doors
They used our own planes our people to kill
And now the evil is trying to hide in the hills
Now they are trying to kill us with our mail
But no matter what we Americans will prevail
We the People are very hot under the collar
The People will now blow you out of the water
We are behind our President heart and soul
Behind him all of the way to kill evil is our goal
I have said some of the things I wanted to say
I will say much more on many more days

The Twin Towers

I have wrote many poems about the New York People
About the Twin Towers and all the very brave people
I watched as the second plane crashed into the tower
I remember the horror of watching the smoking tower
A little later I almost passed out as it started crumbling
I remember feeling a little bit like I was a useless thing
Like a little speck of dust on the side of a big mountain
Wishing I could wrap my arms around a falling mountain
I live in Missouri but I wished all of America could help
And that we could make all the terror and horror melt

New York People

New York people are among the most brave
Whatever they have to do they do not cave
They watched in horror as thousands died
Many rushed to help knowing they might die
Even though they simply could not understand
They all came together and united they stand
The American people are now pulling together
To rid the world of evil to give up no never
We now have the evil running for their lives
A lot of their own people now know evil lies
Evil thinks that it can hide in their caves
But they forget we are the home of the brave
We will not rest until we bring you to justice
Other friendly nations help us do what we must
We are strong as an Eagle and gentle as a Dove
God Bless America and the Land That We Love
Let the New York People know we are so proud
We are here no matter how dark are the clouds

Flight 93

The only difference between all the people on Flight 93
And Twin Towers is they knew that they had to crash 93
They knew the terrorist were going to kill more Americans
So they had one thing they could do to save more Americans
They all agreed to give up their lives to save many more
All they could do is find a way to plow though the door
The terrorist had the door locked so none of them could get in
People had time to call home to tell the trouble they were in
Say their goodbyes and I love you and stormed the pilots door
Got the bad guys and crashed just as God opened up his door

Life In The Country

Life in the Country to this poet is the best way to live
It is the best way to learn Gods way to love and give
If you take the time to observe the many kinds of trees
You will begin to see how lovely they are in the breeze
Then in the hot summer days all the trees provide shade
Their shade saves the life of many creatures every day
They are also a playground for them to play and be safe
Then when their leaves turn different colors in the fall
It is one of Gods way of showing beauty to one and all
Their leaves fall off as winter comes and breezes turn cold
Seeing all the bird and squirrel nests is like finding gold
The thrill of seeing their lovely neighborhood never gets old

More Life In The Country

Here I am writing much more about life in the country
The first one was about the many trees in the country
So it is only fair to write about the land where they stand
Some trees surround life in the country and that is so grand
God made most everything in the country pretty as pictures
God lets the worlds land support all of his living creatures
One of my favorite places to be is under one of those trees
When deer come out under a full moon it is a sight to see
Also watching the beautiful horses and colts run and play
This is just a little bit of life in the country what can I say

More Of Life In The Country

Well here we go again with more of life in the country
I wrote about trees and land they stand on in the country
The scenery alone is more beautiful than you can believe
It makes you want to see all of it before you have to leave
The many rolling hills and the beautiful valleys in between
It is one of the most wonderful sights you have ever seen
Be quiet and you can hear music in those hills and valleys
Then you realize the music is coming from birds and breeze
Add sounds of squirrels rabbits deer and creek water falls
Then you have most all instruments to have a country ball

To Be Some One Who Cares

To be some one who really can care about people
And be some one who realize we are all created equal
Is to be someone who should be in on leading the nation
Not one who thinks they should always be on vacation
But one that thinks they are able to lead with an open mind
And the color of skin or nationality or religion of any kind
Will not have anything to do with how they make decisions
Or who they will call upon to help them complete missions
So the more people who can be someone who really cares
The more likely we will be to make our enemies not to dare
Hurt our great nation because we are all someone who cares

The Rich Land of Missouri

It is made up of great forests and rolling hills
With beautiful wide rivers and big open fields
The American Indians were the first to live here
They had plenty of wild game like rabbit and deer
Missouri is made up of four very different regions
I happen to feel God did this for very good reasons
North of the Missouri river is the northern plains
Along the western border is the western plains
Then comes the beautiful land of the Ozark Highland
Last but not least is the boot heel of Southeast Lowland
Famous Missourians like Boon and Lewis and Clark
Kit Carson and Harry Truman and more left their mark
The State Seal grizzly bears and twenty four stars
State Flag has the Coat of Arms and twenty four stars
Blue Bird is a symbol for happiness and the State Bird
And as for the State Insect the Honeybee is the word
The Flower is the Hawthorn and the Dogwood is the tree
The Fossil is the Crinoid and Black Walnut is the nut tree
The Missouri Waltz is the song the instrument is the Fiddle
Everything I have already had to say is really very little
To describe everything that is great about Missouri State
Is impossible to write in one poem and have it up to date

When Angels Go Bowling

When I was a very little girl growing up
I sat with Granny as she drank from her cup
I loved the stories she told me about herself
Pointing to some things she had on her shelves
There seemed to be a story about each of them
But I think my favorite of all of them back then
Was when she told me about when Angels bowl
She said thunder storms were Angels bowling
Big claps of thunder were the Angles getting strikes
After the game they would all fly off on their bikes

My Grandmother

It is funny how relaxed some people can be
Just by the way they can fall asleep so easily
My Grandmother could set down in her chair
Fall asleep in just a few minutes without a care
She would sleep five to ten minutes at a time
And wake up as if she had nothing on her mind
I always wished I was able to relax that easily
I dearly loved my grandmother so to me it's easy
To wonder why a tiny lady could be so strong
And to me my Grandmother could do no wrong

My Miracle From Heaven

My miracle from heaven is Lillian Grace Mattingly
I know she is a miracle because I am her proud Granny
Nick name is Lilly and like the flower she is heavenly
I thank you dear God for my miracle from heaven
Warm in Mommies tummy is where you stay so safe
Soon you will be out to see your Dads handsome face
Then your Mom and Dad will surround you with love
I know all of these things because I am your Granny
One of these days you will find I will come in handy
I am your Great Grandmother and I have a good plan
And my plan is to try and spoil you as much as I can
But of course we shall keep that plan just between us
As you get a little older we can play an do fun stuff
I write this poem to you Lilly with all my love today
Who knows I may write a book about you some day

With All My Love
Your Great Grandmother

An Angel named Lexi

Lexi Ann Marie Gregg was born one day
She was wrapped in Love what can I say
She looks like an Angel with wings
When she is around my heart sings
The memory of her smiles I will save
So I can bring them back every day
Twinkling stars light up her eyes
Sparkling like stars high in the sky
Pretty and smart just like her sister
And when she is not around I miss her
She is way to brave for her own good
Tell her to climb mountains she would
She is as busy as a bee making honey
She is as sweet and gentle as a bunny
Sometimes she is very funny and wild
Other times a sweet and loving child
You are my Angel whatever you may do
I am your Grandmother and I Love you

An Angel Named Kori Lee

I know a lovely Angel named Kori Lee
If you asked me what she means to me
I would say she is a star in the sky
She is like a moon beam flying high
She walks into a room and it lights
Because her sweet smile is so bright
Kori Lee Morgan Gregg is her name
And making people happy is her game
She is very pretty and very smart
Her sweet little face warms my heart
I some times nick name her noodles
Because she eats noodles by the oodles
She is as lovely as a mourning dove
I wrote this poem for her with love
No I am not her father or her mother
I am her very very proud Grandmother
You are my Angel whatever you may do
Always remember how much I Love you

A Star Named Jake

Jacob David Calfus is his full name
And making us all proud is his game
In everything he does he is a Star
And needless to say he is very smart
He will do great things in this world
While leaving many others in a whirl
He loves and is very good in all sports
Even when the ball is not in his court
He was blessed as far as being handsome
I know this because he is my Grandson
There will be too many girls to mention
All trying hard to get his attention
When he gets older he will fall in love
I am sure she will be lovely as a Dove
I wrote this Poem and put it in a frame
Remember the Love from which it came

Princess to a Queen

A child was born one day in spring
And I think I heard the Angels sing
A Princess is what she looked like
Her sweet smile was warm as sunlight
As she grew it became very apparent
That proud she would make her parents
A Princess named Mellisa Ann Peel
She is in my heart wrapped and sealed
All too soon she was no longer a child
Her personality was spicy and mild
She loves children and they love her
So of course she became a teacher
She went from a Princess to a Queen
It happened very very fast it seems
Her Mother was my very first Child
And she is my very first Grandchild
I wrote this Poem and had it framed
Remember the Love from which it came

The poem I wrote about David Cheney Firefighter
It came from my heart and he is such a Fighter
I am a small part of this wonderful mans big family
Know family I know could be as brave as this family
David and his wife Donna Joy have four great sons
I was blessed to go to a family reunion and I had fun
Not to brag but think our family is second to none

David Cheney-Firefighter

David Cheny is a proud father and husband
To his wife and four sons he is a superman
He has the love and respect of his fellow firemen
And he risks his life every day with all of them
So many people are alive today because of them
David is in the hospital now fighting for his life
Now it is our turn to all pray to God for his life
His wife and sons all pray with all their might
His dear wife and sons all have his bravery
Now all four of their sons serve in the military
David and Donna Cheney love their four sons
Thanking God always for each and every one
Anyone reading this please pray for this family
I know this to be true because I am also family
I write this poem with love and pray for the family

America is in Trouble

By now I am sure most people know what is happening
This nation seams to be crying instead of singing
I am sure the amount of people who believe in God
Out number the amount who do not believe in God
So why is the President allowing no prayer in schools
They do not want us to fly our flag in our schools
Now they do not want us to be so proud of our flag
I happen to be one who has great pride in our flag
Those who do not have this kind of pride make me sad
No wonder so many Americans are so very mad

Have More Compassion

Compassion is something some people live without
They get up and have no idea what compassion is about
They think they are so much better than any one else
They go on with their life thinking only about their self
They come across someone in trouble they walk away
For some reason they have no idea what they should say
I really feel sorry for those who can not feel compassion
It may mean they grew up with the same kind of person
If you know people like that be sure to have compassion
It would also be so wonderful if every person had some

Attitudes Can Change

There are so many different kinds of attitudes
When things are really great you have great attitudes
If things are not great then you have bad attitudes
Little children have different attitudes all the time
They change so often it is very hard to tell sometimes
They may be hungry or wet or may just want to play
But look out those little ones will be teenagers some day
Talk about attitudes there is no way for you to keep up
Do not let it get to you just pour more coffee in your cup
Then try with all your might not to shout loud shut up

Speaking of Attitudes

If you have one of those attitudes that others hate
Then you might want to keep your eye on the gait
If you are in with a lot of people some may get mad
A bad attitude makes some people think you are bad
Whereas if you have a nice attitude you're very well liked
Then your friends will be glad to hand you their mike
You play your cards right you may be the main star
Then learn how to act when you do not feel up to par
That way people will learn to respect and trust in you
Who knows you may begin to love and respect you to

How Right is Right

How right is right is a very strange name for a poem
But this poet has fun being a little strange in my poems
A serious subject but some do not know wrong from right
They know what is right but wrong to them becomes right
Perhaps in their mind they do not know the difference
If some people only knew that doing right makes since
If right is right and wrong is wrong are two wrongs right
OK I told you I have fun being a little bit strange alright
Now that I have proved I can be strange I say good night

Life is like a Game

You have to know the rules to play a game
And hope your partner can do the same
If your partner can not play the game fair
Then you are just floating around in the air
If you can not change your partners mind
Then do not change the rules just to be kind
Find a partner that fair comes natural too
Then your partner will have a partner in you
That makes two who can play by the rules
Be very loving partners and do not be fools
Then you realize life is nothing like a game
And the partner you love feel just the same

Teen Age Children

If only children believed you know wrong from right
Children when they reach their teens think they are right
No matter what you try to teach them they know better
For some reason they know more than all of us together
What ever we do is really dumb really stupid or very wrong
They seem to think that compared to us they are stronger
What amazes me is when they grow up and get their families
All of a sudden they become dumb and stupid and very wrong

Try to be Your Self

You should try to be you and not someone else
It is always better when you can be your self
Because you lose your identity when you pretend
If you pretend to be someone you are not you tend
To forget who you are and lose your personality
That would be tragic because you lose all reality
Of the world as it was before your identity was lost
If you lose your love ones it will be a very hard cost

Little to None

Even people who have little to none
Are able to love as much as anyone
Even if for a living they dig ditches
Than those who have so many riches
Some people let riches close their doors
They think they are better than the poor
There are others who are millionaires
And have compassion and really care
Then some rich people are like sharks
Who feed on the weak to get gold bars
It would be so great if more rich people
Would help children of some poor people
Then many children would have a chance
To excel in school and be able to advance
They would be more able to climb ladders
Than staying on the bottom on teeter totters

Not Naming Names

I do not name names but I think you all recall
There is so many companies breaking so many laws
Even if they get caught they seem to get away with it
And if it was one of us we would be put away for it
But they just seem to get a little slap on the hand
They go back to breaking the law soon as they can
Some celebrities can get by with murder with money
I could sure feed a lot of children with all that money
I could buy air conditioners for those who are dying
I would put a smile on some faces that are now crying

The Bad Wind

Did you ever think about the bad talent the wind has
It has the talent to blow all around and be good or bad
When it is bad it turns hot and cold air into bad storms
It can whip around until all of a sudden a storm is born
It is mean enough to blow over the ocean and raise cane
It loves to blow all around until it turns into a hurricane
Then it can not wait to wreak havoc on shores and beaches
 If it wants to it can destroy almost everything it reaches
When it covers many miles of land it becomes very large
Then it thinks no one but him could possibly be in charge

I Remember When #1

Children could play after dark and have fun at night
Now it is not safe to be outside the house day or night
I remember we used to be able to play hide and seek
With the neighborhood kids all up and down the street
Now the parents are afraid for their kids to be outside
Unless they can be their with them right by their side
But of course that can not happen 24 hours every day
So all we can do is hope we taught them how to stay safe

I Remember When #2

My Brother used to climb the tree outside our back door
He always had a bag of dust just waiting for me of course
So when I came out the back door he took aim to hit me
He blew it because it was Granny who came out you see
He missed the target but he was still in trouble with Granny
Of course I thought it was great that it was she and not me
Because he never hit me with another dust bag ever again
But that never stopped him from using water balloons then

I Remember When #3

One of my brother's favorite things to do for fun
Was to scare his baby sister and then turn and run
Every once in a while my older sister helped me out
We would get him back for scaring us without a doubt
But he would always find a way to get both of us back
The two boys next door helped him to find a new attack
But my big sister was smarter than all of them together
I am bragging I know but as a team we were really better

Where Can You Find Happiness

Many people do not know how or where to find happiness
They think they can find it at a distance but find emptiness
They do not take the time to investigate what they really need
If they only new that sometimes happiness is under their feet
The ground their standing on might be what they are looking for
Happiness is what you find when you go home to your own door
When you open your door and enter your own home your there
You realize happiness is being surrounded by those who care
Love jumps out to you from a mate or children or house pets
I think that is just about as close to happiness as you can get

What is More Lovely

What is more lovely than an Eagle in flight
Or the big full moon over the water at night
The sight of a new born baby in Mothers arms
Or the sight of new born animals at a big farm
Like little baby pigs baby ducks and baby chicks
Then count what puppies and kittens do to the mix
Horses and Cows have their babies and all is fixed
Animal Moms face any threat to save their baby
Human Moms would give their life for their babies
So I ask you what could possibly be more Lovely

There are so many things I would love to say

There are so many things this Poet would love to write or say
So many subjects to talk about it would take more than a day
Since I am a Poet and stubborn I will write about it any way
If you were brave and read my poems I wrote in my first book
Then you may be brave enough to read another one of my books
If you do I am simply stating my own thoughts and feelings
I hope some of you share some of my thoughts and feelings

Turning the Corner

When a miss behaving child finally sees how easy
It is to be nice not naughty then nice is what it will be
All they have to do is see how wonderful it is to be nice
Then all of a sudden everything seems to work out right
The same way all through your life everything has a place
If you are not sure where your place is find out just in case
You find yourself turning a corner that does not seem right
Turning the right corner can be as different as day and night
Turn the right corner and who knows you may find the way
To a whole new life where you can be happy every day

True Conversation

Conversations with many people can be fun sometimes
If the subject is about other people then try to be kind
You never know you might be the subject of conversation
So you want the other people to have very kind information
True conversation about politics is almost unrealistic today
Both parties seem to think their way is the only right way
If both parties could find a way to get on common ground
This nation could make progress dancing to the same sound
They could form a band that all the people could understand
Every nationality and all people could be United We Stand

The Good Wind

The good and bad wind is like the good and bad witch
It is not very hard for you to figure out which is which
The good wind is the complete opposite of the bad wind
It can blow gently through tree tops unlike its ugly twin
All the animals and insects make lovely music together
It travels and picks up more sounds with the nice weather
In the summertime the wind helps to cool everything off
You can really appreciate gentle wind when playing golf
And sitting in the ball park hoping your team will win
That is just a tiny part of what happens with good wind

What Do You Do About What To Do

A friend called me on the phone the other night crying
I asked her what in the world happened are you dying
Oh I am so sorry I did not mean to scare you so much
I set down with my cup of coffee and was very touched
As her story unfolded she wanted to know what to do
Seems her two year old got mad and hit her with a shoe
Did she hit you so hard you did not know what to do
I am sure you were glad it's her shoe and not your shoe
Next time you will know what to do about what to do

I Still Worry About America

Everything we have always had pride in is being taken away

I am sure that most Americans want our values to stay

I do not know why the president and congress lets this happen

What ever happened to the majority wins what ever happens

It looks to me like these people do not know how to say enough

I know how to say enough is enough and it is time to get tough

Our children should be able to recite the pledge of allegince to the flag

People and the military men and women should be able to fly our flag

That is just one of the reasons why they fight with their life to protect

They go to war to protect freedom and life so our flag we should protect

So Much For Fair Play

When you are trying to teach your child fair play
It will not make much since by the end of the day
There is so much news that tells them another story
What they listen to on the news makes them worry
Even some of their favorite stars can not play fair
They wonder why if their stars can not play fair
Then why are their parents making them play fair
About all you can do try to make them understand
To live their life honestly they have to make a stand

Wonderful Times at the Lake

My Mother and Father retired down at the Lake of the Ozarks

Little did they know they made paradise at the Lake of the Ozarks

Their whole family just fell in love with all of the beautiful lake

I know all this because I am part of the family at this lovely lake

We loved to fish and ride in the boats and the kids loved sailing

They loved to sail past the lake house and show off their sailing

Then when the Moms were watching they would try to go slower

It never dawned on them that all of us Moms knew it was slower

They also did not think we new about other things they were
doing

They did not know we had our spies watching what they were
doing

Wonderful Times at the Lake#2

When my husband and I and our two children headed for the lake

We had a hard time getting everything together that we had to take

We took plenty of groceries so Mom and Dad was not out so much

They were on a fixed income so we did not want them to be out much

After all they made it possible for all the families to vacation for free

After packing our clothes and two kids the dog and cat out of the tree

Did I tell you about the dog and cat always goes with us to the lake

They love it as much as the rest of us do and the dog swims in the lake

The cat loves to try to catch birds and give squirrels a really good scare

It is great because I can watch it all while I am up high on the stairs

Wonderful Times at the Lake#3

One day at the lake my husband told me he could fool the deer
I did not believe him so he said tonight I will see some deer
So about one hour after dark he said come on lets go for a walk
I thought he had lost his mind so I said maybe we should talk
He was determined to prove he could walk into a herd of deer
So big brave me I said Ok if you're sure you can find some here
So then we started up the hill on the gravel road very slowly
He said take four steps slowly and stop and four more slowly
Then we heard more steps but they were not from our feet
They got our sent snorted and ran terrified so I excepted defeat

Men and Women Fighting Together

Men and women have been fighting together for a long time now

To make sure those bad guys can not win so they should take a bow

They have the same values about protecting our people and country

They work all over the world to keep children from being hungry

There is no way they can get to all of them but they keep on trying

I just wish the rest of us here at home would try to keep on trying

Keep on trying to save their marriage and take care of their children

If that is impossible they should fight together to care for their children

After all it is not their fault that their marriage fell apart it is theirs

For their sake they should fight together to let them know you both care

Why Not Listen to Your Heart

One of the most important sounds in the world is your heart

You should listen to your heart then your brain may get smart

Even the smartest people would be better off if they listen

No matter how smart you are your heart has the smartest mission

Your heart can take your intelligence all the way to the very top

Think about it without your heart brains are a lot like dust mops

The heart puts feelings in your intelligence so the brain stays clean

With out compassions and feelings the heart gets slow and mean

So if you want to feel right about your decisions listen to the heart

It would get your heart and intelligence off to a really good start

To my husband my children my grandchildren and great grandchildren

My All Grown Up Daughter and Son

I know you all think your children are the best in the world

Most people with children think theirs are the best in the world

Mine both grew up in the music world when they were very young

Their band broke up and went different ways but were still young

Both married and went on with their lives and had two children each

Their marriages fell apart but their children still had two parents each

My daughter had a girl and boy my son had two girls and all are the best

Our grandchildren and great granddaughter now a big sister are the best

My husband and I made it through some bad times but now we are blessed

To my husband and all of my children and grandchildren I say God bless

Lillian Grace Mattingly

To My Lovely Lilly

Here I am at one of your moms many baby showers
She has so many presents to open it will take hours
It is not yet time for you to grace us with your presence
And you already have so many beautiful baby presents
You are in your Moms tummy staying warm and safe
And your Mom and Dad have named you Lillian Grace
That makes Your full name Lillian Grace Mattingly
Your parents' names are Mellissa and Brian Mattingly
I know you are one of Gods Miracles made from love
You will be just like your Mother as lovely as a dove
Your Father will be wrapped around your finger for life
To keep you safe from any harm will be his job for life
God blessed me and let me be your Great Grandmother
And by letting me be your Mothers loving Grandmother
And also by letting me be your Grandmothers Mother
You must be very confused by now but that is OK
We will all be here to help you understand every day

You can call me Granny
I love you with all my heart

85

Do Not be Afraid

Do not be afraid is something that is very easy to say
Most all kids tell each other not to be afraid every day
Just to get them to do something they are afraid to do
So if they do and do not get hurt then they will do it to
Which shows how some kids take advantage of other kids
I wish we could protect our kids from these types of kids
But the best we can do is teach them as much as we can
So they can hold their own against all of them man to man
Then they could find a way to walk together hand in hand
Do not be afraid is said by all of them as they shake hands

News Good or Bad

We turn on the news never knowing if its good or bad
I can not count the times when I turn it on and it is bad
So it is turned off but you know you will turn it back on
So you may as well get it over with the first time it is on
Sounds funny some times but maybe it is about you or yours
Not likely but something bad may have you closing doors
There is so much bad stuff going on here as well as over seas
The troops are worrying about us here at home and over seas
I can not speak for everyone but I think we have had enough
If I was young enough to stand up and shout enough is enough
I am too old to be a fighter to young not to agree enough is
enough

I Love Horses

When I was a little girl I dreamed about horses
At night I would hope I would dream of horses
Sometimes I did and I was upset if I woke up
I got upset if I was daydreaming and woke up
To make matters worse next door they had a pony
And the boys were selfish about sharing the pony
And I would go to bed crying because I had no pony
We could not afford to have or take care of a pony
But when you're a little girl and in love with horses
The word afford means nothing when you love horses

Tornadoes

Tornadoes are such sneaky little storms
They can pop right out of another storm
A Long funnel that sneaks out of a cloud
It can be a very dark and angry dark cloud
It can also be a every beautiful white tornado
They may be beautiful but are still bad tornadoes
They are known to destroy a whole big city
Then lift back up in the cloud in another city
Only to drop back down to kill and destroy
Their only mission is to just kill and destroy

Mike and Cindys Farm

I love to go down to Mike and Cindys farm in Kansas
My daughter Cindy and Mike her boyfriend loves Kansas
I love to go there because it is such a very lovely place to be
From the sliding glass window at the house you can easily see
The beautiful big pond where you can sometimes see the deer
The big field next to it you can see a herd of beautiful deer
Then when you look to the right you can see the two horses
Cindy goes out to see them I swear she can understand horses
It is even more scary that the horses seem to understand Cindy
Even more magic is that Mike loves and understands Cindy

Our Border Collie Dog Tinny

Our border collie did not realize she was actually a dog

She did almost everything we did but we forgot to say dog

So she grew up thinking that she was one of us and so did we

She would sit at the table and play dice and waited for me

When it was her turn I would put the dice right in front of her

 I said your turn she picked as many dice as she could usually four

Toss them on the table and we would say save these four toss again

She gathered the other two and happily tossed both of them again

Everyone would clap their hands and say good girl Tinny you won

She got so excited she would fall off of her chair because she won

Another Wonderful Dog Story

We had another great dog who did not know he was a dog

We named him Prince and I forgot to tell him he was a dog

Our kids were much younger then and Prince was also a kid

I taught him how to play hide and seek with both of the kids

I took him in the kitchen and taught him how to hide his eyes

Then while the kids ran to hide I made sure he hid his eyes

When the kids were hid they would let out with a tarzan call

He ran and his feet started spinning till he got to the hall

He found Cindy in the closet behind some close and drug her out

Then he found Chuck under his bed and he also drug him out

He found My husband too but he decided not to drag him out

Tricks of Our Kids

Kids can think of some strange tricks to play
Our son could think up some dandy tricks to play
And of course a lot of them were about his sister
This little trick took a little time to get his sister
She had two cheer leader pompoms up on the wall
That night Chuck attached a string to the wall
It went from his bed to his sisters pompoms
That night she went to bed and he shook pompoms
She screamed for me and said something is wrong
Pointed to the pompoms said something is wrong
Then we heard Chuck Giggling and it was all over
We laughed as he showed how he moved them over

Back to Mike and Cindys Farm

I was not kidding when I said I love to go to Mike and Cindys
I would love to spend more time there with Mike and Cindy
There are so many things I have not seen yet I hope I can soon
When I finish this book I want to go back and see the full
moon
They also have a very tall deer stand I would love to go up in
Of course I would have to have a lift at my age just to get in
I would also love to go hiking like we did when I was younger
Of course if I tried to now I better pack a lunch or die of
hunger

My Husband Jack

My Husband was only seven days from being seventeen
When his father said he could join the Army at sixteen
As a teenager he was getting into to much trouble at home
So his father gave permission to make the army his home
So for the next few years that is where he called home
To this day he swears that was the only thing that saved him
And now he swears that would save a lot of young men
He said the Army is the only way he could except discipline
Men and women would do better with military discipline

My Husband Jack #2

Jack spent nineteen months over seas in battle in Korea
The ship he was on was destroyed on the way to Korea
They transferred and was saved by a Swedish Hospital Ship
They were never told exactly what happened to their Ship
He went on to serve nineteen months in battle in Korea
He was on one of the Anti/aircraft Guns there in Korea
He about lost his hearing because of all of the very loud noises
Almost froze to death in summer uniforms and had no choices
He was lucky to make it though these problems with his life
Not counting all of the battles he had to fight to keep his life

My Husband Jack #3

Jack was back state side one week before his 21st birthday
He went with a friend of mine so I did not meet him for days
The guy I went with was to sure of himself so I backed off
He said I had to marry him not ask me to so I really backed off
I told myself no man was ever going to tell me what I could do
I was stubborn about him trying to tell me what I could do
Then one day I was sitting on the porch with a girl friend
A car pulled in the drive and there was Jack and my friend
They walked up to the porch I could hardly keep eyes off him
We shook hands I could tell he felt the same way I felt for him

My Husband Jack #4

Lets see I think we left #3 with me on my front porch

Right after my friend and Jack showed up on my porch

We shook hands and knew right then we were together

As we looked at each other we knew we were forever

I was still only 17 and he just turned 21 but I did not care

I always said no man tells me what to do he would not dare

I was so in love I would have flown to the moon with him

He was so in love if I wanted to he would have said When

He would have found a way even if he had to sprout wings

We were so happy and in love we felt we did have wings

Oh Well I Am Stubborn

I really am pretty stubborn and I admit I am
And what ever I am doing I do the best I can
So if I am doing a project it has to be my way
When playing a game win or lose it is my way
I love to make lovely wax flowers with my hands
And they need to be completed by me and my hands
If I am decorating a cake it needs to be my way
So if I am writing poems it has to be wrote my way
If it is a bad poem I have me to blame what can I say

Printed in the United States
by Baker & Taylor Publisher Services